High-Performance Habits

A crash course on how to achieve high performance in your organization

TABLE OF CONTENTS

INTRODUCTION

In a world that is fast-paced, perfectionist, ambition-driven and headed to the hilt, the motivation to join the bandwagon and be all shades of prosperity, is hardly a breath away. As such, it would be foolhardy to remain or be pleased to aim for indolence, mediocrity and being less than perceptive in the real sense of the world. This winner-takes-it-all mantra has permeated every walk of human endeavor - business, religion, politics, health, science, and the likes, with precision and perfection being to the order of the smallest nanometer. In science, miniaturization of gadgets and the achievements of hitherto impossible feats like head transplants, have taken center stage and are keeping the world agape. In business, disproportionate and unprecedented wealth has become the lot of an insignificant few, under the aegis of smart thinking and a shrewd business strategy. In politics and diplomacy, life-changing and far-reaching policies which have had spiral effects on the entire world stage have been promulgated, because of astute and erudite brains which have made it their lot to contribute enormously in that field. In religion, the deity of God and the elements of spirituality are commonplace and easy to grasp because of the strength of spiritual energy and effort being exerted in that direction.

From the foregoing, it would seem like an oddity and a great disservice not to be a partaker of this promise of prosperity and furtherance of the civilization effort the world has to offer today. As such, there are certain high-performance habits that you must imbibe to be an integral part of this moving train.

WHAT IS HIGH PERFORMANCE?

According to analysis by Brendon Buchard, there is no doubt that we all want to be our best but not just during short bursts or when we need to be at our peak or possible best. We want to live and maintain our full potential, to reach and sustain what is called "high performance." From this sentiment expressed here, the definition of high performance is:

The ability to succeed beyond standard norms over the long-term.

As a decisive factor, it goes way beyond becoming the best and operating at full potential. It also involves the science, business, as well as the art and wisdom of remaining there. In some circles, high performance may have outgrown certain definitions.

Some opine that high-performance is simply about achieving better than expected results in a sustainable way that leverages your unique high-performance pattern. To such people, high-performance is a game everyone can play.

According to them, high-performance experiences are not those that produce excellent results. Although excellent results may be an occasional outcome, to define high-performance in that kind of manner would place the experience beyond the reach of all but the gifted few. It is easy to harbor the personal illusion that we could all do excellent work if we wanted to, but for most of us, that is an unattainable dream. Moreover, holding out and making an aggressive and ambitious aim for excellent performance can actually cripple us, keeping us from achieving our best performance with our unique abilities and limitations. High-performance experiences occur within the realm of the personally plausible and as such are truly empowering.

High-performance, according to some psychologists, is a personal thing and everybody can use their personal high-performance patterns to achieve better results.

Unlike popularized peak-performance techniques, the definition of high-performance is relevant for all people, regardless of educational level, experience, age, gender, ethnicity or opportunity. It draws on each individual's unique experiences of high-performance so that he or she can consciously replicate the process in other situations. Any company that equips its employees to produce their own "better than expected" results will see across-the-board improvements. In addition, these improvements will surpass the results of a few isolated and high-up, miracle workers.

Indeed, not only do studies of world-class performance have very little information to give us about how ordinary people produce unexpectedly good results, the fact that we think they have something to teach is often tiring. For instance, most of the techniques promoted in popular books and magazines are peak-performance techniques.

By definition, peak-performance techniques are hardly sustainable. Even the people who promote these methods cannot sustain them. They just use them to speak for a particular athletic meet, a particular performance, or a particular event, more or less to put up a show. The popular press does not and cannot describe the whole process as we do in identifying High-Performance patterns. Only the peripherals that their eyes can see and the mind can perceive are given. Without a detailed explanation, it will be hard for the reader to understand the incredibly disciplined, sustained practice and preparation needed to create the foundation that allows peaking techniques to work. Moreover, without such a foundation, most peak-performance techniques are of limited use.

Your high-performance pattern is already within you.

It is best to utilize that, that is within, to get better results.

World-class results ought to be an occasional by-product of your high-performance approach.

It is the sustainable way.

A HIGH - PERFORMANCE ORGANIZATION

Lots of new research has discovered that the main ingredient in high-performance and growth is found in the psychology & culture of an organization rather than in the mechanics or the empirical. So the important work is in shifting the mindsets, emotional states and behaviors to a psychology that will create and deliver performance, of course of a higher than average quality. However, most businesses focus the vast majority of their energy, attention, and resources, on the mechanics. The collective psychology of people is, of course, the culture.

Culture, like a brand, is misunderstood and often discounted as a touchy-feely component of business that belongs to the human resource department. It is not intangible or fluffy; it is not a vibe or an element of the office décor. It is one of the most important drivers that have to be set or adjusted to drive long-term sustainable success and performance. It is not good enough to have an amazing product and a healthy bank balance. Long-term success is dependent on a culture that is nurtured and alive. Culture is the environment in which a strategy and brand either thrives or dies a slow death.

It can be likened to a habitat for success. It has to be deliberately designed and genuinely nurtured by everyone from the CEO to the least placed. Ignoring the health of your culture is like allowing the aquarium water to get dirty. That is why it is so important to focus and work on culture. But it is an area that is often neglected or poorly managed.

Studies have shown that culture is integral to business success. Going by a survey, which involved 84% of more than 2,200 global participants in the 2013 Culture, and Change Management Survey by Booz & Company, it was easy to infer that culture is critically important to business success. However, there is a marked difference between the way companies view culture and the way they treat it. Less than half of the participants in the survey saw their companies effectively managing culture, and more than half said a major cultural overhaul was needed. Interestingly, 60% of C-suite executives see culture as a bigger success factor than either strategy or operating models.

In his latest book The Culture Cycle, Professor James L. Heskett of Harvard Business School, concludes that effective culture can conveniently account for 20-30% of the differential in corporate performance when compared with culturally un-rooted, if one may, competitors. Even more remarkable were the findings of Kotter and Heskett's landmark study. It documented results for 207 large U.S. companies in 22 different industries over an eleven-year period. They reported that companies that managed their cultures well saw revenue increases of 682% versus 166% for the companies that did not manage their cultures well – stock price increases of 901% versus 74% – and net income increases of 756% versus 1%. These results are staggering and highlight the impact of culture on performance and the bottom-line.

Kotter and Heskett found that strong corporate cultures facilitate adaptation to a changing world, valuing highly, employees, customers, and owners, and encourage leadership from everyone in the firm. So, if customers need change, a firm's culture essentially forces people to change their practices to meet the new needs. In addition, anyone, not just a few people, is empowered to do just that.

Success Factors

According to a five-year study by the HPO

Center in the Netherlands that reviewed 290 academic and management publications and gathered data from 2,500 organizations in 50 countries, High-Performance Organizations share 35 clear characteristics which always appear in five distinct groups.

There was a clear relationship between how well an organization scores on these high-performance indices and its financial performance. Revenue growth was increased by an average of 10%, profitability increased by 26% and Total Shareholder Return by 23% in High-Performance Organizations compared with non-High-Performance Organizations.

Other non-financial performance was also better in the High-Performance Organizations including, higher customer satisfaction, customer loyalty, employee loyalty and quality of products and services than their less able counterparts.

These positive correlations were found in every industry, sector, and country in the world. In fact, it pays to be a High-Performance Organization.

Management Quality

The first and foremost factor that determines whether an organization becomes and stays a High-Performance Organization was identified as the quality of leadership and management of the organization.

In a High-Performance Organization, leadership maintains trust relationships with people on all organizational levels by valuing employees' loyalty, showing people respect, creating and maintaining individual relationships with employees, encouraging belief and trust in others, and treating people fairly.

Managers of a High-Performance Organization

live with integrity and are a role model by being honest and sincere, showing commitment, enthusiasm and respect, having a strong set of ethics and standards, being credible and consistent, maintaining a sense of vulnerability, and by not being self-complacent.

They apply decisive, action-focused decision-making by avoiding over-analysis. At the same time, they foster action-taking by others.

High-Performance Organization leadership coaches and facilitates employees to achieve better results by being supportive, helping them, protecting them from outside interference, and by being available.

Management holds people responsible for results and is decisive about non-performers by always focusing on the achievement of results, maintaining clear accountability for performance, and making tough decisions. Managers of a

High-Performance Organization develop an effective, confident, and strong management style, by communicating the values and by making sure the strategy is known and embraced by all organizational members.

Openness and Action Orientation

The second factor concerns characteristics that not only create an open culture in the organization but also focuses on using this openness to take a dedicated action to achieve results. Management values the opinion of employees by frequently engaging in a dialogue with them, and by involving them in all important business and organizational processes.

High-Performance Organization leadership allows experiments and mistakes by permitting employees to take risks by being willing to take risks themselves and seeing mistakes as an opportunity to learn. In this respect, management welcomes and stimulates change by continuously striving for renewal, developing dynamic managerial capabilities to enhance flexibility and being personally involved in change activities.

People in High-Performance Organizations spend much time on communication, knowledge exchange and learning, in order to obtain new ideas to do their work better and make the organization completely performance-driven.

Orientation for the Long Haul

The third factor indicates that long-term commitment is far more important than short-term gain. Moreover, this long-term commitment is extended to all stakeholders of the organization, suppliers, clients, and the society.

A High-Performance Organization continuously strives to enhance customer value creation by learning what customers want, understanding their values, building excellent relationships with them, having direct contact with them, engaging them, being responsive to them, and focusing on continuously enhancing customer value.

High-Performance Organizations maintains good and long-term relationships with all stakeholders by networking broadly, being generous to society, and creating mutual, beneficial opportunities and win-win relationships. A High-Performance Organization also grows through partnerships with suppliers and customers, thereby turning the organization into an international network corporation.

The leadership of a High-Performance Organization is committed to the organization for the long haul by balancing common purpose with self-interest, and teaching organizational members to put the needs of the enterprise as a whole first. They grow management from their own ranks by encouraging people to become leaders, filling positions with internal talent, and promoting from within.

A High-Performance Organization creates a safe and secure workplace by giving people a sense of safety, (physical and mental) and job security, and by not immediately laying off people until it cannot be avoided, as a last resort.

Consistent Improvement and the Innovative Spirit

The fourth factor is very much in line with a trend that has been keeping organizations busy for the past two decades: continuous improvement and innovation.

This starts with a High-Performance Organization adopting a strategy that will set the company apart by developing many new options and alternatives to compensate for dying strategies. After that, the organization will do everything in its power to fulfill this unique strategy.

It continuously simplifies, improves and aligns all of its processes to improve its ability to respond to events efficiently and effectively. It eliminates unnecessary procedures, work, and information overload.

The company also measures and reports everything that matters, so it rigorously measures progress, consequently monitors goal fulfillment and confronts the breakdowns. It reports these facts not only to management, but also to everyone in the organization so that all organizational members have the financial and non-financial information needed to drive improvement at their disposal. People in a High-Performance Organization feel a moral obligation to strive continuously for the best results.

The organization continuously innovates products, processes, and services, and thus constantly creates new sources of competitive advantage by rapidly developing new products and services to respond to market changes. It also masters its core competencies and is an innovator in them by deciding and sticking to what the company does best. It keeps core competencies inside the firm and outsources non-core competencies.

Quality of Staff

The fifth factor addresses workforce quality. A High-Performance Organization makes sure it assembles a diverse and complementary management team and workforce. It recruits staff with maximum flexibility to help detect the challenges in operations and markets, and takes advantage of opportunities.

A High-Performance Organization continuously works on the development of its workforce by training them to be resilient, innovative, and flexible, letting them learn from others by going into partnerships with suppliers and customers. It inspires them to work on their skills so that they can accomplish extraordinary results. It also holds them responsible for their performance so they will be creative in looking for new productive ways to achieve the desired results.

Creating an Intentional Perfectionist Culture

A performance culture is not an accident, does not occur naturally, and requires constant vigilance to maintain and build. It is a deliberately designed living system of mindsets, processes, incentives, behaviors, leadership, and values that are applied with discipline and commitment. Implementing a performance culture is not a short-term fix, and it cannot be done without the total commitment of the leader and the executive team.

What many companies don't realize is that there are a number of practical "tools" (concepts and techniques designed to change the way individuals think and act) and processes that are proven to increase both the individuals' and the company's future success, and to build and sustain a strong customer-centric culture.

Companies with strong performance cultures think innovatively in everything they do and are constantly searching for better, or more effective ways, of doing things. The optimal outcomes are achieved when each person in the organization channels their creativity and actions toward business growth, people development, an empowering and supportive culture, providing innovative tools and processes for effectiveness and excellence.

Strengthening consumer and customer focus, accountability for results, teamwork and sense of urgency, along with instilling an entrepreneurial, winning spirit, are the keys to achieving success. A High-Performance culture cultivates engagement, enthusiasm, challenges people to take risks in a safe environment, fosters learning, and encourages independent thinking.

People are the most important drivers of outstanding performance. Great people do great things and build outstanding businesses. That is why your major focus should be on the development of your people. The effectiveness of your people can be increased exponentially as they gain exposure to excellent tools and processes, and selectively incorporate and utilize them. These include leadership, management, and technical tools. Staff, managers, and leaders should be encouraged to create, explore, and devise new strategies to develop further leadership and technical skills.

It is the leaders' role to provide people with the tools and resources necessary in order to open minds to possibilities of innovation. For innovation to thrive, it must exist in a culture that energizes and ensures that creative thinking is constantly occurring. Creativity, curiosity, and a genuine openness, are essential for breakthrough innovation. Creating a culture of trust where risks can be taken without a culture of blame and perceived failure is valuable as long as the people benefit through learning and discovery.

It is crucial to nurture an innovative spirit among team members. They should display combinations of creative zeal, problem-solving, risk-taking, and teamwork. Team members need to share in the past successes and not be afraid to address mutually past failures using effective communication methods that do not assign blame.

The only thing of real importance that leaders do is to create and manage culture. If a laid down culture is not managed, it fails to manage the organization, and it is difficult to ascertain the extent to which this happens.

A true vision for a business rests on hinges of both purpose and values. The power of vision is at its best when it comes alive in the people of the organization and they live out the vision.

They become passionate about what they do and why they do it, and perform at a higher level. The business goals must, of an essence, align with this foundation. Without a clear foundation, a business will never be truly intentional and strategic. Therefore, it is better to stand for something beyond simply increasing profits.

PERSONAL HIGH-PERFORMANCE CHARACTERISTICS

The definition of success and high performance is a diverse concept and one that remains unique to each individual. Determining what it means to you, and developing long-term goals, are therefore important steps towards achieving happiness, while you must also be willing to make lifestyle changes and re-evaluate your entire outlook on life.

Be Prepared to Make Sacrifices

On a similar note, you may well be forced to make sacrifices in your quest for success, as any goal that is worth achieving are unlikely to be easily obtainable. The so-called law of sacrifice states simply, that you cannot obtain something that you want without being willing to give something up in return, so you must, therefore, be prepared to sacrifice a life of excess and material possessions in order to be successful in your career.

Maintain a Fit and Healthy Body

According to a growing number of philosophies, there are a number of daily lifestyle choices that can help to create the perfect balance between physical fitness and mental agility. There are numerous studies that have proven the link between the two and it is increasingly clear that regular exercise is a key motivator of enhanced mental performance. Therefore, if you wish to develop the necessary stamina to achieve personal and professional success, a physically fit body is pivotal.

Invest Only in the Pursuit of your Goals

While financial wealth may not be the most

appropriate measure of success, it can certainly be used to fund personal and professional development. With this in mind, it is important to spend money on the development of your career or business, rather than simply investing in material possessions that do little more than not just create a superficial image, but also sometimes incur inherent costs, like taxes on special goods like cars. Making these spending decisions is a key part of chasing success, as it forces you to consider your goals and how much you value their accomplishment.

Befriend Positive and Successful Individuals

Having a diverse and mixed group of friends is fine, but it is imperative that individuals within your social circles share a similar outlook to work and professional success. If you have friends who have a tendency to draw focus and distract you from your work, for example, one may ultimately need to make a choice between pursuing success and settling for your existing lifestyle. If the idea of eliminating people from your life makes you feel uncomfortable, ask yourself if a true friend would risk your long-term happiness by actively preventing you from achieving your goals.

Commit Your Goals to Paper

Whether accepted or not, the power of the diary lies in subtle psychology. Often applied to short-term goals or daily tasks that require completion, this type of list provides an actionable schedule for an individual that enables them to tick their progress as they proceed. This can provide reassurance that you are achieving your goals, and being productive within a given time bracket, and committing your long-term goals to paper may help you to remain focused and motivated during more difficult times.

Never be intimidated

Pursuing success in your chosen profession can be extremely challenging, primarily because you will no doubt, come across intimidating and purposeful individuals who are striving to achieve similar goals. You cannot allow these individuals to undermine or overpower you, as this will put you at a disadvantage and force you to feel inferior to the competition. While you must always respect competing individuals around you, it is important that you remain fearless and back your talent to succeed ultimately.

Don't Entertain Complacency

One of the biggest obstacles to long-term success is complacency, which can easily set-in after positive feedback or the attainment of short-term goals. You must strive to use these achievements as a springboard for more and more however, and rededicate yourself to the cause with renewed vigor. A classic example would be a footballer Cristiano Ronaldo, who, despite emerging as one of the best players in the world, continues to commit himself to a punishing daily fitness regime that pushes him on and on towards self-improvement.

Work harder than your Competition and Those Around you

While you can only control your own efforts in the pursuit of your goals, it is important to remember that those around you also determine your success. When competing with others for a specific goal or prize for example, you must do everything within your power and leave no stone unturned if you want to attain success. At the heart of this is your level of dedication to the cause, as making a commitment to work harder than those around will ultimately afford you a critical edge.

Make a Commitment to Achieve Every Single Day

Although waking up one morning with a proactive and positive outlook is to be encouraged, it means little if you are unable to commit to this every single day. Recommitting to your routine and the pursuit of your goals is crucial to achieving success; otherwise, the pressures of everyday life can divert your focus. While this requires tremendous drive and strength of character, it will ultimately empower you to be successful over a prolonged period.

Choose a Positive Attitude

While there are some who would rather use the fear of failure as a key motivator, it is more likely to create obstructions that deter one from success. Instead, it is far better to be proactive and adopt a positive attitude in everything that you do. Given the variables that can influence your chances of achieving success, it is important that one takes charge of personal outlook and use positivity as a way of identifying opportunities.

Develop an early and Consistent Wake-up Routine

While recent studies have suggested that enjoying eight hours of sleep each day may actually be counter-productive to your levels of mental agility, it is still important that you develop a consistent cycle of sleep. This enables you to become an early riser who wakes up at exactly the same time each day, which makes it far easier for you to optimize your time and develop a productive schedule. Therefore, while the rest of the world is still snoozing in bed, you can be taking decisive action towards empowering your body and mind for the day ahead.

Learn from Failure

While failure is considered a teacher of important life lessons, drawing from painful and disappointing experiences is far easier said than done. In fact, it requires an ability to decipher the exact lessons that we can learn from each individual failure so that we can apply these in the search for future success. By confronting the issue squarely, and identifying exactly where things went south, you can take decisive and actionable steps towards ensuring that the same mistakes are not made again.

Take up a Challenge and Undertake Difficult Tasks

You cannot succeed in life without first achieving personal growth, which demands a willingness to accept and overcome difficult challenges. It is only through overcoming obstacles that we are able to learn and develop important life skills and values, and it is these attributes that will equip us to obtain success. By challenging yourself and confronting difficult tasks, you can also change your mindset concerning the possibilities that life holds.

Measure Success in Happiness Rather than Wealth

The modern generation of employees is increasingly motivated by factors other than wealth, with job satisfaction, benefits and empowerments, all key considerations. This also represents a shift in the way that people measure and define success, as defining it in pounds and pence or dollars and cents, only leads you to chase consistently a higher amount with ever achieving true satisfaction. This can be counter-productive, so be sure to create a clearly defined vision of success and understand precisely what it means to you.

CORE VALUES OF HIGH PERFORMANCE KNOWN TO MAN

Perseverance

This can be defined or described as the consistent and dogged determination employed in getting a seemingly difficult task done.

Life is challenging or hard. It will be normal to go through challenging times throughout our journey in life. At school, at work, in our relationships, even in church, there will be situations and circumstances that would test our patience and resolve. At times, at the end of such tests, something nice and glorious will present itself.

It is understood that perseverance is a virtue that everyone needs if we are to be successful in life. The grit to brace up against all odds and endure the constant brick walls that tend to resist an advancement towards our goal, is something that should be a part of everyone's lexicon if victory is to be our lot.

It is however unfortunate that this virtue may be in short supply, as everyone is in the fast lane, and patience is hardly obtainable in life's situations in recent times. It is because of this malady that shortcuts are often sought, which unfortunately, are fraught with lots of disadvantages, inferior alternatives, and lots of exposure to danger to the risk of reputation, money, time, and even life. A popular saying goes that shortcuts cut short, and it could not have been more aptly put.

Being consistent is a virtue that requires faith and belief, conviction and ambition. Without these qualities, one would most likely crumble or succumb to the slightest opposition. There has to be an unwavering faith in the cause one is pursuing along with the implicit belief that success would be sure. An unwavering faith, and a strong belief, will ensure you have the motivation to continually strive towards your goal regardless of what obstacles you come up against.

Conversely, if you don't have the belief that you can accomplish a particular goal, then the likelihood is that you'll quit, meaning you won't ever succeed, which in turn reinforces and substantiates your theory that you couldn't succeed anyway. The danger in this is that challenges are copious and dense along the pathway of life, and it is easy to develop this as a habit, and could develop into a life philosophy. When it does, it breeds insecurity and low self-esteem, which could get to the extremities of suicide and suicidal thoughts.

Having a deep inner belief that you can succeed simply means that there isn't the slightest doubt, and that the temptation to give up will never be overwhelming, even though it may be there. You will be equipped with the mentality and belief that your success is just around the corner. Yes, there may be major challenges, or possibly defeats along the way, but because you have a belief that you will eventually succeed, you will revise your game-plan, tweak your strategies, keep moving forward, and therefore, dramatically improve your chances of success.

Perseverance is a virtue that is nurtured and cultivated. It is done by first having a clear-cut definition of one's purpose and path in life, as well as the aim that is needed to be reached. There also has to be a systematic plan to achieve this to go with it, as well as the implicit faith that whatever happens, the commitment to stay true to the cause will not drop. There also needs to be a timeline or period during which one is expected to achieve the objective. It may be days, months or even years. It does not really matter whether or not the aim is achieved during that period, but most people who have done that, have found themselves achieving their goals around that period, earlier or later by a little time. When choosing this period, promise yourself to keep working towards the objective regardless of the obstacles and hindrances that present themselves on the course of the journey, and do not quit or stop before the allotted time. When the deadline that has been set arrives and per-adventure, the goal isn't achieved, it will be best to re-arrange and reorganize but NEVER to quit. Note the obstacles that come as progress is made. This will help in identification and help in creating pathways to overcoming these obstacles. It will also be right to confide in people who are more experienced in the particular field. They may be parents, relations, siblings, or even mentors. These people will use their wealth of knowledge to chart courses of progress which one may never have imagined possible. They can also act as checks when one seems to be derailing from the pathway.

In a commitment to achieving an aim, there will always be distractions which can come in any form. It could be in form of friends, advice, a habit, a relationship, or something that will have the potential of taking one off the beaten path. It is best to identify them and avoid them to remain focused. It is also important to establish daily habits that will be helpful in actualizing your dream. For example, if one aims to be richer by 30,000 dollars before the year runs out, the easiest way to achieve it would be to put away a certain amount per day or per month that would add up to the amount, or approximately, by the turn of the year. It would also be wise to avoid situations that tempt one not to commit to that habit, like frivolous spending and the likes.

As the saying goes, -little drops of water make the mighty ocean, consistent, and constant, and little drops of effort, will culminate in a large result at the end of the day.

Benefits of Perseverance

The Merriam Webster Dictionary defines perseverance as *"continued effort to do or achieve something despite difficulties, failure, or opposition.*

There are times when giving up on a particular goal seems like the next best and logical thing to do because of the challenges being faced. But there are also people who see a task as unusual when it succeeds at first touch, and are actually unhappy when this happens, or have a premonition that the feat achieved will not be a long-lasting one. The onus will therefore be on us to re-strategize and refocus to achieve the desired goal as many times as it would require for victory to be sure. The ability to do this has an increased likelihood that our dreams and aspirations will be met with success because, just like a popular saying goes, the universe is fashioned in such a way as to fall in love with the dogged fighter.

For example, a child who desires to learn how to ride a bike without the help of a tutor or guide, will try to balance his weight on the bike while pedaling and maintaining constant speed. This isn't a day's feat, and he may crash from the bike a couple of times, fail to get the pedaling right, and at other times, fail to propel the machine into motion. But with constant approach, and a mind to succeed, he will get his acts together, and it will not be a surprise to see him being in perfect control of the bike in weeks or months to come. That is the power of perseverance.

According to findings, as encapsulated in the EHE Newsletter, some goals may need us to make drastic changes to our lifestyles or generally step out of our comfort zones. It could be loss of weight, learning a new language, learning a new skill set like swimming or some form of sport, quitting harmful habits like smoking, or even getting out of debt. The underlying factor there is, is that it is never an easy task, but with determination and persistence, it is usually doable.

One of the benefits accruable from this is the feeling of accomplishment and satisfaction that trails the success we desire. There is this overwhelming feeling of empowerment, confidence, and pride, that is enrapturing at such times, and there is the desire to want to experience them again and again, hence the need to persevere.

In the words of Barbara Frederickson in her work titled "The Role of Positive Emotions in Positive Psychology," she states that positive emotions help counteract negative emotions, promote creativity, broaden the mind, and open individuals up to new possibilities and ideas. They may also have long-lasting consequences, by helping us to build enduring physical, social, intellectual, and psychological resources to draw from. When these feelings that come from success becomes a habit and way of life, it is easy to take ownership of our lives and chart a course for ourselves knowing that something is achievable, and it opens a new vista of opportunities for even greater success.

On the other hand, when one is unable to persevere, negative emotions become his or her lot and this is usually difficult to overcome, causing problems for the individual's mental health. However, the cheering news is that the virtue of this habit can be imbibed over time, and this can begin when one chooses a goal he or she is passionate about, and the zeal in the individual would provide the motivation needed to go through obstacles and challenges as they come. Many times, achieving a large goal may comprise of smaller sub-goals that would add up to the larger one. For example, someone learning to drive a car must first master the workings and intricacies of the gear system, the steering wheel, as well as road signs and of course driving etiquette. The small successes achieved in these sub-goals would then be the needed motivation towards the compound vision being actualized.

By developing perseverance, you can prevent the negative cycle of emotions that comes from failing to meet your goals. This can help to prevent the negative actions and consequences that often result from negative emotions. According to careful analysis by psychologist Jake Ducey, there are other reasons why quitting shouldn't be in one's lexicon, and they include the following:

- When quitting becomes a habit, it has the tendency of making one compromise on what is important, and at the end, it leaves an air of mediocrity, which is dangerous. It develops into nonchalance, and from there; life becomes insipid, which may lead to depression and its attendant problems.

- Sometimes, why we fail repeatedly may be that the right and timely questions have not been asked or the right materials have not been consulted. When it is hit, then boom! The gold is struck.

- In the most practical sense of the word, there is no such thing as an excuse to quit. This is because what we term as an excuse, -age, height, health, sex, and all what not-haves, served as a springboard to others if we research properly on people with seemingly so-called setbacks. So in the final analysis, that excuse does not exist!

Michael Jordan made it to the NBA Hall of Fame after being "not good enough" for his high school basketball team. Steve Jobs became a millionaire at 21 years old. Bethany Hamilton had her arm bitten off by a shark and is still one of the best female surfers in the world. Oprah Winfrey was fired from her television-reporting job because they told her she wasn't fit to be on screen. 27 different publishers rejected Dr. Seuss' first book but his story has changed today.

- Lack of perseverance has a way of creating self-judgment and negative vibes around the individual. It also causes inner conflict because the individual isn't true to his or her inner desires. That goal was desired, and that was why it was embarked upon in the first place. Something was aborted when it was given up on.

- It is possible that we sometimes give an exaggerated picture of our situations to ourselves. The truth is, it isn't as bad as we tell ourselves it is! It would be nice to look at the sunny side of things, and persistence would be easy to imbibe.

PERSEVERING WISELY

Now, it isn't just about waiting and trying everything one knows in the book, or doing the same thing and expecting a miracle to happen, or manna to fall from the heaven when we are past the dispensation of the children of Egypt. This wise act also has to do with not just work, but wise, and smart work. It is about re-strategizing, modifying, pressing on, re-inventing new ways of doing things, and all it takes. There are three major ways people persevere, although the degree of success and the time lag in achieving this varies and matters. People are persistent on a course in three distinct ways:

-Trial and Error:

This is the cheapest and easiest way. This is comprised of series of trials and failures on a particular process that could be repeated or varied. For example, a mechanic who is determined to investigate the source of a fault of a car can do it by working on all other allied parts of the machine. The snag in this is that it may be found, but it spends a lot of time and energy that could have been channeled somewhere else.

-Joining an Educated Community or Group:

This could be the next best thing after trial and error. Sometimes it doesn't work out as envisaged during the trial and error stage. One may decide to join a group or community, where the solution is perceived to be present or pointers to the solution of a problem. By networking and interaction, answers to an issue may be realized. This is more directed and focused than the trial and error method. It may or may not involve financial investment.

-Hiring a Mentor or Coach:

This one is more direct and instant. One gets under the tutelage or mentorship of someone who is well versed and experienced in the field for an agreed period. It usually involves fees, honorariums, and payment for the transfer of knowledge in various forms and names. The results are instant and the issue is tackled immediately.

Most people are usually on the brink of success. It, however, takes sheer grit and persistence to continue until success is attained. Here is a curated list of people who persisted and succeeded at the brink of success, and when giving up was the best option:

Jim Carrey

When Carrey was 14 years old, his father became jobless and it became rough for the family. They moved into a van on a relative's lawn. Who could tell that the young comedian who was dedicated and perseverant at his craft, mailed his resume to The Carroll Burnett Show just a few years earlier. Once, at age 10—took an eight-hours-per-day factory job after school to help make ends meet.

At age 15, Carrey performed his debut comedy routine on stage in a suit his mom gave him—and totally flunked, but it mattered little. The next year, at 16, he left school to focus on comedy full time. He moved to Los Angeles shortly after, where he would park on Mulholland Drive every night and envision his success. One of these nights, he wrote himself a check for $10,000,000 for "Acting Services Rendered," which he dated for Thanksgiving in 1995. Just before that date, he made his big break with the flick Dumb and Dumber. He put the deteriorated check, which he had kept in his wallet the whole time, in his father's casket.

Tyler Perry

Perry's childhood was as rough as they come. He suffered physical and sexual abuse growing up, got kicked out of high school, and attempted suicide twice — once in his pre-teens and again at 22. At 23, he moved to Atlanta and took up menial jobs as he started working on his stage career.

In 1992 he wrote, produced, and starred in his first theatre production, "I Know I've Been Changed," was somewhat created by his difficult upbringing. Perry invested his life savings into the show and it failed abysmally; the run lasted just one weekend and only 30 people came to watch. He kept up with the production, working more odd jobs and often slept in his car to save costs. Six years later, Perry finally broke through when, on its seventh run, the show became a success. He has since gone on to have an extremely successful career as a director, writer and actor. In fact, Perry was named Forbes' highest-grossing man in the entertainment circles in 2011.

Abraham Lincoln

This die-hard was born in 1809. Abraham Lincoln is famously known for being the 16th President of the United States. He championed the cause of equal rights, and he was an arrowhead in blazing the trail for slave freedom in America. But Lincoln didn't start out successful. He failed many times before attaining the highest office in the land.

In 1832, when he was 23 years old, Lincoln lost his job. At the same time, he also lost his bid for

State Legislature. Just 3 years later, at the age of 26, the love of his life, Ann Rutledge, passed away. Three years later, he lost his bid to become Speaker in the Illinois House of Representatives.

In 1848, at the age of 39, Lincoln also failed in his intention to become Commissioner of the General Land Office in Washington D.C. Ten years after that, at 49, he was still defeated in his quest to become a U.S. Senator. Of course, through all the personal, business, and political failures, Lincoln almost, but did not give up.

In 1846, Lincoln was finally elected to the U.S. House of Representatives where he drafted a bill to abolish slavery. In 1861, at the age of 52, he secured the office of President of the United States and has since become one of the most famous failures to hold that office in the United States. His face ceremoniously appears on the U.S. five-dollar bill.

Stephen King

Stephen King was almost penniless and struggling when he started his writing career. He lived in a trailer with his wife who was also a writer—and they both did multiple jobs to support their family while pursuing their skill. The poverty was to the level they had to borrow dresses for their wedding and had telephone bills tallying on their finances. Stephen King got so many rejection letters from publishers for his works, that he developed a system for collecting and saving them. In his book titled "On Writing," he recalls, "by the time I was 14...the nail in my wall would no longer support the weight of the rejection slips impaled upon it. I replaced the nail with a spike and kept on writing." He received 60 rejections before selling his first short story, "The Glass Floor," for $35. Even his now best-selling book, Carrie, wasn't a hit at first. After dozens of rejections, he finally sold it for a meager advance to Doubleday Publishing, where the hardback sold a miserly 13,000 copies—not good at all. Soon after, though, Signet Books signed on for the paperback rights for $400,000, $200,000 of which went to Big Steve. Success was now history!

J.K Rowling

J.K. Rowling had just gone through a divorce, was living on government aid, and could barely afford to feed her baby in 1994, just three years before the first Harry Potter book, "Harry Potter and The Philosopher's Stone," was published. When she was marketing it, she could hardly afford the cost of a computer, talk about the cost of photocopying the over 85,000-word novel. Therefore, she manually typed out each version to send to publishers. It was rejected many times, until finally Bloomsbury, a small London publisher, gave it a second chance after the owner's eight-year-old daughter fell in love with it. Today, the work is worth hundreds of thousands, if not millions of dollars, the book has gone on to be made into a movie that has been an all-time hit.

Harold Sanders

Colonel Harland Sanders was always in and out of jobs throughout his career. He first started cooking chicken in his roadside Shell Service Station; at 40. It was the time of the Great Depression. His gas station didn't actually have a restaurant so he served dinners in the quarters he attached to his home.

Through the next 10 years, he perfected his recipe, a pressure fryer-cooking method for his presently famous fried chicken, and moved onto bigger locations. His chicken even got an accolade from food critic Duncan Hines, the much acclaimed Duncan Hines. However, as an interstate project passed through Kentucky town where the Colonel's restaurant was in the 1950's, it took away important road traffic, consequently losing his clientele and the Colonel was forced to close his business, ultimately retiring and of course broke for the most part. Worried about how he was going to live on his paltry $105 monthly pension check, he set out to find restaurants who would franchise his secret recipe at a nickel for each piece of chicken sold. He drove around, sleeping in his car, and was rejected more than 1,000 times before finally finding his first partner. Today all that is history.

Oprah Winfrey

The name "Oprah" such a household name now, didn't believe she was going to be this famous. She has gone through and dealt with a lot throughout her public life. There has been criticism about her weight, racist comments and nuances, bothering questions about her sexual orientations and preferences, just to name a few — but she never let it get in the way of her ambition and drive. She can now think of the several issues she had and smile because of her success story in the light of all she overcame successfully.

Growing up, it was reported that Oprah was a victim of sexual abuse and was repeatedly molested by her cousin, an uncle, and a family friend. Later, she became pregnant and gave birth to a child at age 14, who died just two weeks later. But Oprah persevered, went on to finish high school as an honor student, earning a full scholarship to college, and working her way up through the ranks of television, all the way from a local network anchor in Nashville, to an international superstar and creator of her own network. Oprah Winfrey is currently worth around 3 billion dollars.

Warren Buffet

Warren is currently the Chairperson and Chief Executive of Berkshire Hathaway, a financial services company and commonly called the sage of financial wisdom. Each time he refers to the acquisition of his company worth over 200 billion dollars, he refers to it as a "200 billion dollar mistake." He says this because it was once a struggling textile mill. Even though he managed to turn the fortunes of the company around and make something profitable of it through the years, he feels he could have invested that time and energy on other sectors. The success of Berkshire Hathaway was still enmeshed in struggles and repeated failures anyways.

Shawn Carter (Jay-Z)

From an early age, Jay-Z had a penchant for rhythm. However, his swift rise to stardom didn't just happen overnight. He was faced with several hurdles along the path to ultimate success. For example, in 1995 when Jay-Z tried tirelessly to strike a record deal, not a single label would sign him, to the point he almost gave up. It led him to establish his own record company called Roc-a-fella Records with partners Damon Dash and Kareem Biggs.

After being turned down by so many labels, and eventually starting up his own record company, Jay-Z worked tirelessly to strike a distribution deal for his first album's release. He was also faced with serious challenges and rejections. Eventually, he successfully negotiated a contract with Priority, later releasing his debut album entitled, "Reasonable Doubt," which would eventually go on to hit platinum.

Jay-Z met with many real-time failures, not just challenges in the course of his musical career. Those failures weren't just at the beginning of his career, but the beginning did a lot to highlight the tremendous amount of resistance he had to deal with to achieve success. And, even at the peak of his career, Jay-Z was charged with allegedly stabbing someone at a record release party. He was tried, pleading not guilty, but later pleaded to a lesser criminal misdemeanor, resulting in three years of probation.

Considering that Jay-Z's background was that of the slums of Brooklyn, New York, and grew up in debilitating poverty, he faced many failures and roadblocks in his life. But he never gave up. No matter what happened to him, no matter what failures he faced, he pushed through, growing as a person and maturing to become a better individual.

Henry Ford

Almost everyone knows Henry Ford for the Ford

Motor Company, one of the most successful automobile companies of all time. However, what most of them don't know is that Ford failed two painful times before that abruptly resulted in financial hurdles, prior to successfully launching the present rebirth of his company.

Failure isn't new to the man Henry Ford, but he also didn't give up. Yet, when we think about Ford, the failures don't come into the picture because all it took was just a one-time success. However, in 1899, at the age of 36, Ford formed his first company, the Detroit Automobile Company, with backing from the famed lumber baron, William H. Murphy. That company eventually filed for insolvency.

He made a second attempt in 1901 when he formed the Henry Ford Company, which he ended up leaving with the rights to his name. That company was later renamed the Cadillac Automobile Company. However, it was Ford's third try, with the Ford Motor Company, that hit the proverbial nail on the head. But he was always contemplating giving up at such painful points.

After that, we all know the story. Ford went on to rebrand the automobile industry, pioneering not only the Model T and the assembly line, but also the concept and notion of an automobile in every home. Driving became a "thing," and subsequently, Ford's Model T went on to sell over 17 million units.

Thomas Alva Edison

This is one name that we have all heard and will never go out of fashion as long as there is an electric bulb in this world. This famous American is known for failing over 10,000 times to invent a commercially sellable electric light bulb, but he didn't give up. When he was asked by a newspaper reporter if he felt like a failure and if he should give up after having gone through over 9,000 failed attempts, Edison simply replied in the epic manner that has stood the test of time: "Why would I feel like a failure? Moreover, why would I ever give up? I now know definitely over 9,000 ways an electric light bulb will not work. Success is almost within my grasp."

He was not just acclaimed a failure in his inventions; his teachers also branded him as being "too stupid to learn anything." He was also fired from his first two job positions for not being productive enough. However, Edison, through his failures, is also the greatest innovator of all time with 1,093 United States patent rights to his name, along with several others in the United Kingdom and Canada. This is someone who refused to give up no matter what.

It's said that in his early days, he attributed his success to his mother, who pulled him out of school and began to coach him herself. It's opined that it was because of his mother, and how completely she believed in him, that made him swear not to disappoint her. His early fascination for chemical experiments and mechanical engineering became a platform for a future that was incredibly bright. His company, GE, is still one of the largest publicly traded firms in the world, continually innovating across virtually every shade of the business.

MANAGING YOUR TIME

The Mind Tools Content Team defines this as the process of organizing and planning how to divide your time between specific activities. Good time management enables one to work smarter – *not harder* – so that you are done in less time, even when your schedule is overwhelming and pressures are high. Failing to manage your time damages one's effectiveness and causes stress.

It may seem counter-intuitive to dedicate precious time to learning about time management instead of using it to get on with your work, but the benefits are large, and include:

- Greater productivity and efficiency.
- A better professional reputation.
- Less stress.
- Increased opportunities for advancement.

- Greater opportunities to achieve important life and career goals.

Kristar Haav and his team have carefully curated this list of tips that can enhance the judicial use of time, as is typical of experts and high performing people:

1. There ought to be a way of measuring how much time is spent on each activity per day. This helps us prioritize and get the best use of the number of hours allocated to each day. Do you know the Pareto principle? It is an effective tool for managing time. This will be discussed in the subsequent chapter.

2. Let there be a clear-cut result that is expected at every meeting or appointment.

3. Try to allot specific periods for time spent on a particular task or project. This makes the work efficient and helps you to be a

good manager of this asset.

4. Let the entire activities of the week be planned on Sunday to have a clear program of events throughout the week.

5. There should be a to-do list for each day. This grants focus, which is so important in managing time.

6. Keep track of accomplished tasks on a daily or weekly basis as the case may be, to monitor progress and utilization of time.

7. Be sure to complete the most daunting tasks in the freshness of the morning, when the faculties of the body are rearing to go. The less important ones can come later. It helps more to be done in less time.

8. Insulate yourself from distractions of any kind.

9. Multitasking used to be a strength, but researchers have found out that it is

counter –productive.

Say No to Procrastination

Though a task seems so important, and doing it can save a large chunk of your time, you may still want to put it off for a variety of reasons. Perhaps the task seems overwhelming or unpleasant.

This is the point where you need to know that procrastinating that daily task of today only increases tomorrow's task and waste your time. DO THAT TASK NOW!

Try breaking down tasks into smaller segments that require less time commitment, and result into specific, realistic deadlines. If you're having trouble getting started, you may need to complete a preparatory task such as collecting materials or organizing your to do list.

Managing Time Wasters

Your time could be impacted by external factors imposed by other people and things. You can decrease or eliminate time spent on these activities by:

- Using a voice mail and set aside time to return calls.

- Do not engage yourself in small unproductive discussions. Stay focused on the reason for a call.

- Remain standing while talking on the phone. That way, you are more likely to keep a conversation brief.

- Set aside times of the day for receiving calls and let others know when you are available.

- Establish blocks of time when you will be available for visits.

- Set aside a specific time to view and respond to your mail and e-mails, but don't let it accumulate to the point that it becomes overwhelming to sort.

Sleep

Sleep is, and should be, a quintessential part of one's day. It is critical to brain and body function, and allotted good timing and ordering in the day's program. In fact, several studies have described the importance of sleep in relation to not just productivity, but the quality of life, and it will be apt to describe some of them here to justify the importance of sleep to everyday life.

According to a scientific research undertaken by Paula Alhola and Paivi Polo-Kantola, in 2007, they made deliberate and in-depth inquisition at the causes and effects of sleep deprivation, and came out with the following conclusions:

-that sleep is important for thermoregulation, tissue recovery, body restitution and energy conservation.

-that sleep deprivation impairs cognitive

functions of the brain as well as working memory.

According to an independent study by a group of pharmacists who sought to establish a relationship between hours of sleep and academic performance, in a work entitled "Sleep and Academic Performance," it was discovered that the amount of sleep was proportionally positive to the grade performances of the students under review.

Statistics arising from the effect of sleep driving, which is a direct fallout of insufficient sleep goes as thus (in America):

It turns out that sleepy driving is a concern that plagues about 60% of adult drivers as 168 million Americans have driven a vehicle while feeling drowsy in the past year alone. Alarmingly, 37% of adult drivers, or 103 million people, have actually fallen asleep at the wheel before. 13% of those who have actually fallen asleep at the wheel has done so at least once a month. 11 million drivers admit that their sleepiness has caused an accident or near accident. 100,000 police-reported crashes are the result of driver sleepiness every year, according to the National Highway Safety Administration, and that is severely under-reported since it is currently very hard to assess sleepiness as the cause of a crash.

Researchers have illustrated the need for consistent, quality sleep, with a simple experiment that shows the impact of sleep debt. When healthy people are forced to stay awake continuously for one or two days, their waking state is eventually interrupted by short episodes of involuntary sleep. Test subjects are incapable of avoiding them. Moreover, other adverse consequences can be observed at the same time:

- declining cognitive performance
- poor memory consolidation

- impaired attention and decision-making
- slow reaction time

The slow reaction time can be one of the most dangerous effects, as it is not only the cause of many car accidents but also some of the biggest maladies in history, like the Exxon Valdez Oil Spill, Chernobyl, Three Mile Island, and The Challenger.

Scientists have observed, over longer periods, that a chronic lack of sleep:

- negatively affects learning and memory
- reduces immunity against diseases
- shortens lifespans

Intellectuals assert that the relationship between time and money, which has been tested and proven, makes it possible for anyone to reap the advantages of time management efficiently by managing time properly. The advantage of managing time efficiently can be seen as a kind of art. People spend very little time with fewer efforts in understanding the intricacies of judicious time use. For some, there is praise for trying, but by giving up, they made a vital mistake just on the sign of difficulty. The importance of advantageous use of time will provide some insight that certainly changes our belief systems.

BENEFITS OF TIME MANAGEMENT

Managing time is an activity that neither is elaborate nor demands too much. It is just a knowledge of how to be dedicated to implementing a prepared schedule. In addition, it's even more important to balance day to day activities for better results, and even success. The implemented change never being an easy task, it becomes little more persistent when the benefits are understood. It will bring you a positive response. The benefit of good time use is not just important for boosting a career; it has a significant impact on one's personal life. A wise scheduling decision is involved and leads to self-discipline as there are many advantages of punctuality. The advantage is that the scope of time management is not restricted to day-to-day affairs. A daily and well-coordinated plan can translate into a lifetime of deliberate and scheduled achievement. Some gains of effective time use include the following:

- It creates a hunger for achievement

Achievement of one single task is different from achieving back-to-back successes. A series of repeated successes become ours when we make a deliberate effort to sustain it, not just get it. Discipline and working on oneself are compulsory. The communication tools are available in a variety of ways. Time can be used effectively by sometimes outsourcing duties, and even using technology as a sacrifice to more pressing matters. For example, web conferencing can be used when absence is inevitable. The good news is that with little investment, it pays off hugely. The achievement comes with hardworking and dedicated behavior. Everyone needs to adopt time control if they desire to have a taste of success.

- It Reduces Stress

The reduction in stress level is the main content of judicious time utilization. One can even relax while working. Stress leads to disruption of work schedule and this, in turn, can never provide best results. The result will come undoubtedly but no one can say it will be best or worst.

- It Creates Room for Recreation

It is no gainsaying that recreation in this era of 'rush and all work' is a blessing and everybody wants it, but unfortunately, it is only within the reach of a few. There is so much pressure to achieve and achieve until the entire day, month, and year, is choked with activities. But with proper scheduling, events and appointments are properly spaced and timed, and it will be a shock as to how much time will be left for relaxation, which by the way is indispensable to life and health. The workday will be scheduled with reminders and alerts for urgent events. The blessed ones are those who do work on time and adopt a timetable in their life to do day-to-day chaos. The relaxed life and mind gives motivation to human beings and fixes them on the path of success. The recreational activities also give family life a boost. People connect more with their families and loved ones. A good work-family balance is an essential ingredient to all-around success.

- Beams the Searchlight on the Task Ahead

The skill of time control first provides relief from stress and then helps you in focusing on the target and performance in the task. A focused person becomes successful in less time as compared to those who struggle more to hit their target in life. The people who always desire to have successful and stress-free life, always know that it can be obtained and easily too, by keeping a focused view of everything and every step.

There is much duration of life and it brings fluctuation. The key to adopting time management is the ability to predict the results that would come and be able to tweak the situations. Using time well isn't completely rocket science. It only needs one to have the knowledge about how to do it and be dedicated to implementing it within your day-to-day activities.

- It Fosters Self-confidence

Self-confidence is a key psychological ingredient that plays an important role in human life and relationships. Self-confident people always have a better life than insecure persons do. The feeling of confidence is usually attendant with good planning and scheduling, and decisions are taken on time for the betterment of the individual and his work. One business coach opines, "Time management never takes your time, rather provides you extra time." This couldn't have been more aptly put. A person who can do anything with confidence and self-trust, is always a candidate for the next level of life.

• Scheduling points to the goal

Everybody has a burning desire to achieve his/her goal in life. and dreams to lay back and relax after attaining the said goal. Managing time allows you time where it is most impactful. Effective and efficient time control allows humans to spend time on the things that matter most to them. In this process, time management has a positive aspect to perform and people consider the scheduling a better option.

- It Questions and Improves Productivity

The capacity of everybody has been found to be similar. The differentiating factor is in the habits of the individual, and that is what brings about different results. The people who score 100 out of 100 are also humans and not robots; the deciding factor is that they consciously follow their dreams. Noble use of time is in sync with someone's determination to follow it religiously, which questions the former way of doing things, and gears one up for improved productivity. Meetings are listed in an orderly manner in a to-do list. The activities can be set up in a sequential manner according to the most pressing of them, followed by the least important. Productivity is a challenge to face, as the process of productivity puts individuals on their heels.

It's a race which has to be won by all. In all, it is a great thing to adopt but also demands the capacity to handle pressure.

HOW TO PRIORITISE

There are times one can be busy, activities and all, yet there is no sense of direction and purpose in all of the labor. It is possible to be active, yet gaining next to nothing, and an honest audit would reveal that the time expended is more or less a wasted one. One of the causes of this would be the fact that there was no sense of distinguishing urgency and importance to duties. Everything was attacked as they came, and midway into it, it would become so mixed up and frustrating that the reasonable thing to do would be to pause and, with a deep breath, do a cursory assessment.

High performing individuals have a sense of prioritization in their dealings. There is a graduation of urgency and allotment of energy to each activity on the schedule and this is what prioritization is all about. Prioritization is defined by the dictionary as the ability of a manager or administrator to deal with issues, activities, appointments, and schedules, in their order of importance or urgency.

Sometimes, it is possible to be enmeshed in activities that give a marginal sense of accomplishment at the expense of others that are supposed to bequeath full-time value. Either because the latter is not recognized, or has not been fully understood for what it is and the potential in it, time is wasted, energy is expended on all fronts, and the individual or outfit becomes the worse for it.

Prioritization has rules and tie-posts. To prioritize effectively, there are certain pertinent questions that must be holistically addressed. They include the following:

- What are your values?
- What are your goals?
- What are your responsibilities?

- What is the impact of the activity on the organization or outfit?

There are specific points to keep in mind to help one prioritize assignments in order to be a high-performing individual. They include:

- Place value on what is important to you.

Values should guide one's overall direction in life, and they provide the foundation for one's goals and priorities. Goals are defined as impact-oriented results or accomplishments one has set out to achieve within a period or no period at all.

- Let your responsibilities also tell heavily on your priorities.

A student has the responsibility to attend class, complete assignments, learn the class material, etc. An employee has the responsibility to go to work, work well with others and be productive. Your responsibilities to your family can have a tremendous effect on your priorities. In fact, let the responsibility define the priority. Finally, as a rule of thumb, to be successful over the long haul, your priorities must be impactful and have lasting value.

- Never dismiss your priorities when bombarded with other people's priorities.

Life is full of avenues, turns and twists. It is very good to be of assistance to someone, but it will be counter-productive to allow someone else's program to swallow up yours. Someone may bring an issue to you seeking help; this issue may be a priority for him but not necessarily for you. By working on his priority, you spend time that could be spent on your own priorities. Of course, the topmost snare will be the friendship you share which you may not want to lose or jeopardize, so his matter may be worth your time. This is not to discourage rendering help; in fact, helping others should be a priority. However, it doesn't mean one should automatically place a higher priority on the requests of other people above your own priorities. For example, if you have a major examination in the morning, but your friend wants to tell you something that is less important tonight, it would be wise to suggest to him that you talk about it tomorrow after your exam. In other words, there is need to prioritize your need to study above the frivolity of talking gibberish.

It is important to grasp the fact that urgent issues, whether yours or someone else's, does not mean they are important.

Many people have a hard time recognizing the difference between urgency and importance. The point is, that the heightened enthusiasm often associated with urgency counterfeits itself as importance. Don't be fooled: it is better to work on the most important things first and remember that urgent issues are not necessarily important issues.

Several Psychologists and social scientists have done extensive work on this concept of time management and the most effective ways to achieve scintillating results.

THE PARETO PRINCIPLE

The Pareto Principle is one made popular by the Italian economist Vilfredo Pareto. It specifies an unequal relationship between input or investment, and the results gotten from such investment of whatever kind. Also known as the 80-20 rule, it states that in business or in human endeavour,

80 percent of the result is accounted for by 20 percent of input or effort.

For example, the Market Business News site is of the opinion that of a company's 100 products, twenty are likely to represent 80% of profits. The

Principle does not actually stipulate that every single situation has an exact ratio of 80/20. It just puts forward that figure as a typical distribution. Put simply; its message says that a small percentage of inputs cause the majority of outputs. The Pareto Principle is just an exemplification of the fact that the idea of equitable distribution is a farce and is practically non-existent.

In practice, an insignificant number of people or population controls majority of the outcome. This has been seen to be applicable in all walks of life and seems to be true. For example, a research has shown that even mobile phone messages follow the Pareto Principle. Twenty percent of contacts in most people's smartphones represent about 80% of all messages. A cursory look at your social media page will show that the number of likes is always from the same miniscule number of close friends.

The Cambridge Dictionary also explains this rule as meaning that a small amount of work or resources is responsible for a large number of results. It simply shows that life isn't fair. Why then should you fail to prioritize by selecting the top 20% task to get a good result?

Applications of the Pareto Principle

The Pareto Principle helps us realize that most outcomes are the result of a minority of inputs. Therefore, if…

– Twenty percent of workers account for four-fifths of the results, we should focus on rewarding them and motivating them. Alternatively, we could send the other 80% on tailor-made training courses.

– 20% of customers make up 80% of our income; we should channel more resources towards satisfying these customers.

– 20% of bugs are responsible for 80% of crashes; our priority should be fixing those bugs first.

We should first determine where that 20% can be found and then focus on them. We would subsequently get a better return on invested time and resources.

SELF-IMPROVEMENT AND OUTSOURCING

Self-improvement

This is another characteristic that cannot be overlooked by high-performing individuals. There is the constant drive and urge to learn new things, increase capacity and knowledge, new skills, as well as newer ways of doing things.

This is the study and practice of improving one's life, especially our career, education, relationships, health, happiness, productivity, spirituality, and other personal goals. Common aspects of increasing capacity include goal setting, motivation, changing habits, improving awareness, identifying one's values and beliefs, and self-actualization.

The first step to being a better person is to totally accept yourself and like yourself for who you are. This is because one of the root causes of insecurities, self-limitations and emotional issues, is having the belief that you're not good enough.

Accepting and forgetting about the things that you cannot change, and only focusing on what you can change, will allow you to put all your energy into the things that you can do something about.

There is no reason why you cannot have, be, do or become almost anything that you want.

"Like the air you breathe, abundance in all things is available to you. Your life will simply be as good as you allow it to be." - Esther Hicks

It could not have been more aptly put, because life is all about evolvement and change, both on the personal and global fronts. The ability to move with the tide and fit in properly is one that every successful and high performing individual holds close to his chest and does everything to accomplish.

OUTSOURCING

This is another great quality of individuals who are high performers. Because there is so much to do, there is the tendency to overwhelm the schedule and consequently muddle things up. This quality would have been thought to be an offshoot of the prioritization characteristic of highly successful people. The ability to prioritize tells on the tendency to decide what is important for the time being and what isn't. However, the fact that something isn't important now does not mean it won't be in the future, nor does it mean there isn't value attached to it. Sometimes, it would be a wise idea to get two tasks completed at once or in record time. This is where outsourcing comes in.

Outsourcing is usually a business practice

wherein companies or individuals shift responsibility for operations, tasks, and processes, to other companies or individuals to either reduce costs or increase efficiency.

How Does Outsourcing Help?

- Outsourcing engenders Focus

The expansion of the back operations of a company is proportional to the expansion of a company. This expansion sometimes begins to place undue demand on resources, both human and capital, at the expense of the core activities that have made your company successful. When outsourcing is done, there is refocus on the main activities that handed the company its success, without telling negatively on the actual output of the back operations.

For instance, a company that lands a huge contract that will magnificently increase the volume of purchasing in a very short period, will be wise and shrewd to outsource the purchasing.

• Operational Control

Sometimes, operations can run out of control and must be put on the outsourcing list. Departments that may have evolved over time into uncontrolled and poorly managed areas are the best candidates for outsourcing. In addition, an outsourcing company can bring better management skills to your company than what would otherwise be available or done internally, since there is the edge of neutrality and specialization.

For example, an information technology department that has put its hands in too many projects, and is understaffed with a budget that far exceeds their contribution to the organization, will be the best attraction to be outsourced. A contracted outsourcing agreement will catalyze prioritization of their requests and brings control back to that area.

- Improves the Company's Local Capacity

There are cases whereby a large project needs to be undertaken that require skills that do not exist among the staff. On-site outsourcing of the project will, of course, bring people with the skills you need in your company. Your people can work alongside them to acquire the new set of skills.

An instance could be, a company needs to embark on a replacement or upgrade a project on a variety of custom-built equipment, and the resident engineers do not have the skills required to design the required new and upgraded equipment.

The ideas of outsourcing this project and requiring the outsourced engineers to work on-site will allow your engineers to acquire a new skill set.

- The Staff become Flexible

The phenomenon of outsourcing will allow operations, that have seasonal or comeback demands, to bring in additional resources when needed and release them when done.

An example, is an accounting department that is kind of short of extra hands during tax season and auditing periods. When these functions are outsourced, these functions can provide the additional resources for a fixed period at a consistent and reasonable cost.

The bottom line is, as many things that cause distractions, as many things that bear down on time, as many things that are not priorities, can be and should be, outsourced so that the focus can be single, and this is one underlying characteristic of high performing people.

- Outsourcing Reduces Overhead Costs

The overhead cost of performing a particular back-office function has the potential of being extremely high. It would be kind to the company to consider outsourcing those functions that can be moved easily.

Example: Growth has resulted in an increased need for larger space in the office. The current location is very expensive and there is little or no room for expansion.

There have to be simple operations that can be outsourced to reduce the need for office space. Instances include the outbound telemarketing or data entry.

HIGH PERFORMING PEOPLE HAVE A GOAL IN MIND

People who are high flyers operate with a goal in mind. The goal in focus is usually singular and directional. It would be foolhardy and a gross waste of time and effort, to fill the mind and heart with dreams and ambitions that have no concrete bearing and direction to the individual's potentials and abilities. Now, focus is a virtue and that requires strength of will and purpose. There are many things begging for attention, even dreams and desires. A lot would seem attractive and doable once the mind has been set on achieving a particular thing, and before you know it, it has constituted a distraction. But the good news is, it can be checked. Here are some ways one can refocus and sharpen this resolve to zero-in on a particular goal, which has been set:

1. First, it is key to understand what constitutes a distraction and systematically devote effort to diminishing it. It is

important to organize and prepare yourself accordingly before taking on new tasks. While organizing, get rid of distractors so that as soon as you start working, no one and nothing will stop you.

2. For some, music can be distracting but it can also be motivating and inspiring for others. It has the power to relax, cheer up, instigate nostalgic feelings, and even motivate. Therefore, it is a commonly ignored but integral ingredient to focus or to help us focus.

3. Some people are into different genres of music for different applications. It could be rhythm and blues, hip-hop, classical, salsa, you name it, or a specific collection dedicated to elevating focus. Excellence in anything can be achieved through a mixture of features, like determination, a

positive attitude and hard work. Focus is a necessity for success.

4. One of the key poses of distraction is technology and social media. Not only does it chew away at your time, it has a way of shaping the mind in its own fashion, many times away from the original and intended terms of reference. It would be wise to extricate oneself from the addictive grip of phones, tablets, Facebook, Twitter and Instagram when it is perceived to constitute such a distraction.

5. While insulating oneself from people and things that constitute a derail to dreams and visions, it is equally key to find a way to be comfortable and productive when at the main thing.

When you need a place to work, study or read, find somewhere that will not only be comfortable but also have all the previously mentioned features within itself.

It may be a corner of a café, library, an office room, or something else entirely. Your goal is more important than any side frivolities.

HIGH PERFORMING PEOPLE UNDERSTAND THEIR AUDIENCE

Whoever you are and whatever your niche in life, you have a client and an audience whose needs you cater to, and who you depend on for advantage, reach, support and even sustenance. Actually, one's career depends heavily on one's audience and how appreciative they are of one's content. There is always something to sell, and there are always people to buy into it and feed on it. That is why it seems like the world is akin to a cyclic value chain with a lot of links and locks.

One of the characteristics of high performing people is that they understand the audience they are feeding, and know exactly how to satisfy their cravings and to keep them coming back for more. This singular quality, aptly put to use, has the guarantee of perpetuating a successful career and even growing it.

A motivational speaker ought to know the caliber and level of people he is addressing, and he has to justify the fat checks by giving them the right dose of motivational talk to fire them up. What motivates a primary school kid is miles apart from what would ignite a football coach. A football player must of essence, justify the million dollar sign on fees by living up to the expectations of the fans and coaching crew, or else he would find himself jobless by the end of the season, or sold out on loan to a smaller placed side where his skills would be hardly noticed. A pastor should understand the intelligence level, assimilating level, as well as the spiritual level of the audience he ministers to, to reach out effectively to their needs and their betterment.

An in-depth knowledge and understanding of an audience is, in fact, the essential ingredient to running a business or building a brand. Audience analysis is something successful people have perfected and implemented for the betterment of their careers.

CONCLUSION

The quest towards high performance, perfection, and precision is a real and daunting one. May people and as a matter of fact, everyone, enjoys the dazzle and applause that comes with making headlines, breaking records and hitting top list of successful people and all that comes with it. However, the real question is, how many people are ready for the gruel and grind it takes to legitimately get to the top and remain there? The preceding chapters of this book have given a detailed do's and don'ts regarding high performance and consequently, success, because the two go hand in hand.

The universe is made of equal and opposite forces - matter of fact I may say unequal forces -good and evil, success and mediocrity, love and hate, and the likes, and it is unfortunate to note that it is the positive virtue that one has to work hard to attain or achieve. By default and by indolence, mediocrity stares one in the face where there is no detailed drive and motivation to persevere with a goal in mind. There must be a determined effort to manage time wisely, prioritize between tasks, improve one's capacity where needed - if not all the time, outsourcing the threatening tasks, and understanding whom one is dealing with as a client.

Because of the way the world has been fashioned, success becomes an unstable state, borrowing the parlance of the scientists, effort and work must be put in to sustain it, for as long as is possible, else, one returns back to the stable state of underachievement.